Liquid Love

Published by Infinite love. For information, address Infinite Love,
 74 E Glenwood Ave Unit #5873, Smyrna, DE 19977

Illustrated by: Kate Lozovska
ISBN: 9798218796433
Author's Website:
https://infiniteinlove.com/

Contents

1   Introduction

4   Love and Happiness

6   Memories

8   Heartbreaker

13   True Soulmate

18   Our Spot

20   Attraction

22   Quest for truth

24   Light Poem

26   4/21

28   Twin Flame

31   Beauty Untouched

34   La última vez

35   La última vez Translated

36   An Ode to Love

38   You and I

40   Life Support

42   Life Release

43   Still Here

45   369

48   The Final Act

50   Silence Speaks

56   Acknowledgments

Introduction

This collection gathers poems I've written in notebooks from ages 15-22. I decided to name this book *Liquid Love* because, to me, love is fluid. It's an ever-flowing and ever-changing energy that has the power to move through people, spaces, music, words, senses and thoughts. Through the vessels this energy embraces, I have felt a greater sense of what it means to be alive, because this is the very reason I am alive.

Liquid love is a palpable current. It nourishes by seeping through every cell in your being. It floods, opening wounds to memories left drowning. It consumes, grows, purifies, cleanses and carries us even when we find it difficult to lift ourselves. In these poems, I've tried to capture the different forms that love has poured into my life — moments both joyful and devastating, brief and lasting.

Love has appeared in many forms in my life: platonic love, self-love and romantic love. Notably, many of these experiences have been shaped by some amazing people I've met along my journey of life, particularly, with women that I have shared a deep connection with. To each of you, I thank you. Whether you brought me clarity or chaos, comfort or confusion, your presence gave me something real to feel. Something to reflect and expand upon, and to that, I wrote.

I began writing these poems, not with the goal of becoming a poet (although now, I do love this title), but to give a voice to those things I didn't quite know how to express. Through my teenage years, I struggled with depression and other weighing mental health issues. Poetry became a container for feelings that spilled over. During my most vulnerable times, my notebook became my best friend, and my pencil became my sword. They helped me survive, reflect, and remember who I was before the world told me who to be.

This book is not just a collection of love poems. It's a documentation of becoming. Of remembering. Of shedding. Of feeling too much, and then writing it anyway. May these poems find you wherever you are on your journey, and remind you that love — in all its forms — is never wasted. It just transforms.

Love and Happiness

Two key components in life, set out on a quest.
Searching for each other,
nothing more and nothing less.
For they were unsatisfied.
They sought to be tied.

The rush kicked in, so they could find each other
before they died.
Desperation began to unfold.

They longed to fore hold the goal of striking gold.
Having their mind feeling controlled.
Couldn't see the truth,
it's like they were wearing a blind fold.

Blindly thinking each other is what they need.
Thinking if they come together, they'll succeed.
Planting a seed made of greed,
not realizing they already had it all, they both
agreed.

See,

they thought if they agreed to decree this misdeed,
they'd exceed.
Their core was about to explode in a pile of
nastiness.
They kept drawing closer trying to get through the
fuzziness.
Realizing how powerful they could be,
they both earned the trait of cockiness.

At last, they met,
but
they only felt the feeling of loneliness.
They realized they were homeless
and, then overcame sadness.

It was at this time when they'd been robbed of
everything...
that happiness realized it was love,
and love realized, it was happiness.

Memories

Trapped within the emotional memories.
I pray for peace within the darkness.
Locked away in my cage–
unconcerned with the day's festivities.
The ruthless monsters tear away at me so heartless.

At the end of the day
what is there to present?
The mind drifting away into the atmosphere.
Countless times of judgement, so
please excuse me if I'm hesitant.
A cloud of sadness in the midst of cheer.

At times,
it seems easy to give up and let them win.
They charge at my fright.
I'm locked up, but I ain't in no pen.
The hardest time to make it through, is the night.

Falling through the bottomless pit of never-ending
pain,
wandering into the land of the unknown.

People and the voices will have me wondering if I'm even sane.
Holding in my true feelings so they are not shown.

Nobody else does.
So, why should I care?
The pain and the hurt are what I mostly recall.
They have destroyed everything else.
So, what next will they tear?
If I shut everybody out,
who will be there to pick me up when I fall?

I will stand and take my place.
I act hard, never revealing my sensitivities.
Starting to handle my problems face to face,
so I'll move forward, but I'll never let go of the memories.

Heartbreaker

There we stand,
with her heart in my hand.
I,
still remain intact
while the life of her body she lacks.

Walking along the dark path,
planning about the heart I will smash.
Oh,
how she looks at me.

She gives up everything.
I take it, but hesitantly.

Heart beating faster,
caught up in the laughter.
The love for you is not there.
The love between us I do not share.

I will have to do it.
But I don't want to be the cause of the depressing
pit.
Please,

just don't talk.
Let's just travel silently until I end this walk.

Why must you be so loyal?
I'm unhappy but still, your life, I do not want to soil.

Pressure coming down,
I have to do it now.

I take you aside,
trying to hint with compassion.
Oh, how many times have you cried?

Each word piercing a slash.
I can see you falling,
your body is going to crash.
Slashing away
the price to pay for a heartbreak.

My ghost has always been around your presence.
I hoped your tone would lessen,
but it only got stronger
I just wanted to get closer to being a loner.
You're not making this easy.

I'm trying to be distant while you're still trying to please me.

Why must you care so much?
Feelings of delight with my every touch.
I don't want you anymore.
I'm sure you've noticed...
The way I've been acting is hard to ignore.
I want this to completely end.
But
I'd break your heart if I let the message send.

I came into this truth
wanting nothing more but to fall in love with you.
But
for me it never happened.
But
you thought it would be forever,
so your seatbelt you have fastened.

Please stop loving me.
The guilt of a heart breaker makes it hard to flee.
You deserve better.
Is it cold for me to leave you in the dust and say,
"forget her?"

No,

for my heart is too warm.

I'm too weak to let your heart be torn.

For the time being, I'll be back

we can maybe resume this later after I adapt.

To kill you as softly as I can,

I put it on pause.

I guess I will have to be the cause.

Forgive me for everything I have done.

I turn away from society as I accept my shun.

So much happiness within yourself.

Please just lie me on top of the lover's shelf.

The days are approaching.

Locking in the kill with one swift motioning.

Going through the same dance,

love has you in a trance.

I planned my actions.

First,

I will tear away your passion.

Then,

I will rip away your devotion.

I will do this all in one swift motion.
Next,
I will tear up the life in your body.
I will do this easily and effortlessly like it was my
hobby.

Yes,
your love and loyalty I will have to kill.
So,
can you please just remain still?

True Soulmate

Blindsided to the lies you disguised

I'm...

disgusted by the times you were mine.

As I write these rhymes through the lines, I realized

that...

you were never mine.

See it was all a facade,

a distraction.

I put it to the side,

all your baggage,

thinking I could look past it.

This is harassment — the way that you're acting.

I'm embarrassed.

Putting 2 and 2 together, now it's adding up.

Me plus you together was corrupt.

A volcano bound to erupt.

Now,

I'll admit it, yeah, I fucked up.

Look, I'm not a perfect nigga but I'm a worth it

nigga.

So don't play me like I'm a worthless nigga.

I'm the top of the top.

The top of the notch.

You were the top until I got to the top and realized
you're not.
You're not who you say you are.
You had a role and you played your part.
You played with my heart.

See, I knew it from the start that we wouldn't last.
Yet,
I made so many excuses.
Feeling like a prisoner being brought to their
execution.
So, this is how it all ends?
This is how it unfolds?
We were better off as friends,
I just knew it in my soul.

You have me disgusted.
Nah,
I ain't mad at the new nigga you fuck with.
I've adjusted.
I'm disgusted by our discussions.
How do you say one thing but you do another?
How do you hate something when you claim you're
a lover?

Tell me it's a joke so we can laugh about it now.

Thought before I spoke to analyze these sounds–

I feel like a clown about to drown.

And no,

I'm not talking about Pennywise, but this ain't It.

Thinking about all those petty lies and how you just ain't shit.

See,

you dropped a bag of diamonds and gold.

Running away with a heart that you think you stole.

But baby, my love ain't something that you can just throw or control,

shift and mold,

turn off and turn on,

turn warm then turn cold-

No.

This is an experience.

Love so mesmerizing it'll make you delirious, I'm serious.

You ain't just hearing it, you feeling it!

This experience is bewilderment.

So complex it can have you fearing it but,

ain't no fear in it.

It can take all these voids and fill 'em in.

My love is infinite – it'll never end...
regardless of all of your flaws and sins.

So,
even in the end,
I close this book with a grin,
a smile.
I skip back to before we were friends,
before I even pictured you walking down the aisle.
I wave with bliss and say goodbye with a kiss.
You,
I might miss, but I can never come back to this.

So don't try to come back with this greed in you to
take.
Lie awake and live in the bed you make.
Don't hope for fate to open these gates.
Go on dates and live as a snake
I'll be okay.
I'll just listen to Drake.
I'll be...

sharing my bread with those who help me bake,
eating with those who brought me a plate,

learning from my mistakes.
I'll wait...

to share my love with my true soulmate.

Our Spot

Who am I on this lake?

A serene being at peace with my thoughts...

No.

Who else are you going to take?

No meaning with these words left off...

My happy place,
       watching the sun rest.
I see her face
       during these sunsets.

There are no better nights than these.
All of the bittersweet memories...

Remember
those times with me?

When

Heaven gleams
     and light beams
          leaves me...
blinded.

Sun shining,
     moon brightening
         colliding
            then,
                 di-
                     viding.

They say there's nothing new under the sun.

Yet,

I am always reborn under this one.

Attraction

Hey,

I hope this isn't too intrusive:

When I saw you,

my mind became inconclusive.

If you're with someone exclusive

then...

these next lines will only sound illusive.

So,

I'm hoping you can help clear up any confusion.

See,

I think you're beautiful

and,

I'm not just talking about the usual.

I'm talking

about the stuff that makes tulips grow.

That light

that shines within you is truly unforgettable.

And if I

didn't reach out-

it would be unforgivable.

So,

I have to know:

Do I have an opportunity to make this poem of my
fondness grow
or
have I already reached the end of the road?

Quest for truth

Encased within the race of the pace,
where the beating of my heart feels misplaced.
To be loved and love.
This is not enough
without someone to hug.
Constantly craving physical touch,
constantly wondering,
"Where is my one?"
"Did she give up?"

Or have I?

Because I'm hiding behind a disguise.
Face molded into a mask of lies.
Trying to be one of those guys
where I let women swim in by the boatloads.
Having silent competitions of who looks best with
no clothes
and who's the true throat goat.

No.

I don't want to use women like they use tampons.

For one time, to go inside,
get the job done and say goodbye.

I know that ain't what we're really made for.
The creator put us on this Earth to do way more:
to share, give and create love.
Women, men and wherever you feel like you fit in:
we all need it now more than ever.

So why compromise for pleasure when we can get
what's better than better?

Real love.

Light Poem

Dear light,

please guide me right,
as I travel blind with no sight
because my eyes deceive me,
and my mental may choose tricks rather than
treats.
Treat the healing that's needed to take place within
thee,
softly.
One hard blow to this little root might be awfully
costly.
As I journey around the world,
I unlock more places within,
hidden within the inscriptions of decisions I've
made in alternate dimensions.
Afflictions of addictions that contort pain into sweet
prescriptions.
What world do I live in?
All these talks about breaking out of the system,
created by a few that's now afflicting billions.
Sometimes, wisdom can be as draining as viscum.
The reptilian politicians,

all the disappearing innocent children,
the lies about our heritage,
this world as we know it, nearing its end.

Many roles this great stage offers yet,
why is it so difficult to play your part?
Many are graduated scholars yet,
never learned the lessons of their heart.

Where shall we go from here?

Well,
as the light approaches near
I pray that your path has been made clear.
Persevere and alchemize your fears.
For, the light is here.

4/21/24

Maybe a part of her still resides within me...

Remembering as I watch the sunlight dimming.
Those times of our highest memories.

Chasing our dreams,

young and naïve.

Yet, not everything is always as good as it seems.
Just like us, you see what I mean?

But

your passions still live on.

Within my life your fire is still goin'
slow, but strong.

I thank you for your presence
and who you are to me.

Thanks for being a blessing.

Take care, Maddy.

Twin Flame

A hidden treasure within the closet stowed away.

I passed by you every day.

However, our true encounter was a delay.

Or was it?

Because time has a funny way to trick

and when it's divine,

it's even more slick.

Is this it?

That one song on the album I used to always skip,

but now I find out it's the shit!

You felt like a breath of fresh air.

All this time you were there, but I just wasn't aware.

You get me, you see me.

And just when I thought I had nothing left,

you expanded my capacity.

Changed my whole reality.

I mean practically,

we had to meet like that.

How else could we have grown so magically?

Yet, tragically,

how could it end so sadly?

With the match we had, I found it hard not to

attach,

but with the fire we shared, you knew you had to take a step back.
Lifetimes in the past you told me we had crossed paths.
Warning me it would not last, but I paid no attention to that because I just wanted you back.
Then you vanished like the drop of a hat.
It's hard to heal when you're bleeding from a wound you can't see.
Starting to peel back the layers that I know I can't keep.
Internally, the parts of me I hide, are beginning to creep back slowly.
But with you,
my mask was never a disguise,
and you saw straight through those lies,
because you know me.
Teaching me authenticity,
you left
but,
left me wholly.
Our memories are ingrained within my soul,
and those times when I felt so alone,
I remember that you know.

The beautiful painting in the gallery that I've
learned to just admire
instead of trying to take or inquire.
The beauty I found in the dark,
the magic mirror on the wall.
Time can only tell the truth of our hearts,
and if we'll ever meet again at all.

Beauty Untouched

Wandering through this experience,
allowing my eyes to gaze, but nothing too serious.
Because I just tried to frame what I thought was the
perfect picture — it just wouldn't fit.
So,
I find myself back in this exhibit.
Exhibiting bewilderment,
processing the feelings of discontent
until,
I had this fated event.

Is this the beauty in the dark, I've passed by 1000
times?
I've seen you plenty of times before, but somehow
you never caught my eye.
Wow, look at your features!
Look at your glow!
I told myself, "I have to have this now!"
But
something inside of me said, "No."
So,
I thought, maybe it would help if we took things
slow.

Well then, show me all of your work, I said, "I have
to know."
Walking along some paths I've never taken before.
Adventuring with this artist, I thought I knew, but
now have come to adore.

Could you be the picture whose frame could fit?
This question burning inside of me I don't think I
can ignore it.
We share so much love, I must admit.
With all of this chemistry, there must be more!
"Would you be willing to give me your art?" I said.
But ever since I asked that question it seems we got
torn apart.
So, in my head, questioning what I did,
I retraced my steps back to the start.
I was wandering in the exhibit...
Glancing, but nothing too serious,
looking to find a picture that could fit,
processing the feelings of discontent.
Maybe this was it...

Trying to fill a void to a bottomless pit.
Trying to own and control

whatever I could to satisfy the desperate ego.

So now, as I am back at the start,
looking through the lens of my heart, at your art
I've learned to love, experience, and simply
appreciate
the beauty in the dark.

La última vez

La última vez no siempre es feliz,
pero antes de que una lágrima toque tu nariz
piensa en esto para mí:
que suertúdo eres en este momento.

Es esta una nueva vida lo que estás sintiendo?
una oportunidad para un grandisimo, neuvo
movimiento?
pensamiento crítico es el fundamento.

La muerte es un paso a otra vida,
un adiós a todo lo que has conocida,
porque las bendiciones acechan en la desconocida.

Felicidades por todos tus cambios,
llueven milagros de tus labios.

Por ahora tu eres más sabio, gracias a Dios
Amor infinito.

The Last Time (La ultima vez translated)

The last time isn't always happy,
but before a tear touches your nose
think about this for me:
How lucky you are right now.

Is this a new life you're feeling?
an opportunity for a huge, new move?
critical thinking is the foundation.

Death is a step to another life,
a goodbye to everything you've known,
because blessings lurk in the unknown.

Congratulations on all your changes,
Miracles raining from your lips.

For now, you are wiser, thanks to God
Infinite love.

An Ode to love

I feel your pulse vibrate throughout my being.
A force so vibrant, present and unseen.
I am that blade of grass, winding up with the rising
of the morning sun.
Seeing through me like glass, you lift me up as our
consciousness merge into one.
Coating every cell with the rays of your light,
even when I simply inhale and exhale, I know that I
am beautiful in your sight.
How wonderful is your presence to be so purifying
and uplifting?
The distance you'll go for me is purely defying, it's
so healing.
Thank you for reminding me of my purpose:
to protect and nurture it.
Informing me, you are not confined to any one
person.
I accept your pure intent.
I give myself permission to allow your fire to ignite
within me.
On my journey of Ascension, there will be no liars
hidden from these beams.

For your essence requires full truth and
vulnerability.
So, my presence will be a beacon that shines
diligently.
I am eternally grateful to be with you deliberately.
As I give, receive, and appreciate love, infinitely.

- Infinite Love

You and I

Fairy Tales
have been written in your honor.
Large- scale
productions released on worlds beyond yonder.

Your beauty?
A catalyst for war.

Truly,

leaving me quenching,
thirsting for more.

How could I have found you,
when I didn't know I was searching?

Lifting me up from a downing gloom,
I feel your energy emerging.

I appreciate your gift,
for your presence is a present.

Gentle kisses from the bottom of your lips,
this essence feels like blushes from my adolescence.

Now that we have met again,
divinely aligned, truly knowing within:

this is a blessin'.

Just know that as I fly,
my wings are coated with your mind's eye.

For this love shall never die.

It shall always remain between *You and I*.

Life Support

Mourning the death of many
who have not yet left, but are still living.
How much left do I have in me?

With every new beginning, you seem to always be
my end.
Seeking comfort within ending, there you show up
once more again.
The true test of time with all mortal men.

What happens to that little caged bird when you
finally open the door?
How could such freedom be found when you don't
know what to look for?
Plenty of dreams you couldn't ignore, but now
afraid to go out and explore.

Let me cry.
Let me scream.
Let me groan.

As I fly,
I will sing

my song.

I'm just a little bird
and, I don't know where to go.

Let my voice be heard,
I'm trying to make it on my own.

As the night swallows me whole
and I realize I'm all alone:

Light, please just guide me home.

I wanna go home.
I wanna be home.

Life Release

I have nothing except,
I'm waiting to exhale this last breath.
For this will be my everything.
The final sacrifice before handing over my entire
being.
Your nudges
felt like rips of my limbs, splitting of my torso.
Your touches,
as soft as the wind hitting line dry clothes.
How can you be so striking yet gentle?
Your force, so almighty, I *tremble*.
I have worked so hard to hold onto everything I
know.
These grips leaving me scarred.
You,
urging me to just let go-
No.
I must fight back with all the might I possess!
Slowly, taking away everything I could grab, I start
to release my last breath...
Wondering what's next and what my new life shall
be in this death?
I just let go, and release all that I have left.

Still Here

Residing in constant movement
to this language I have become fluent.

Wishes become facts
as they appear in the manner in which they were
presented.
Without question, I act,
giving no ear to the banter proposing limits-
there is none.

Everything is everything.
So, we are all one.
Blessings upon blessings,
you are the sum
to this juxtaposition
of never ending
questions that demand decisions.

Livin'
and
breathin'
in the worlds you live in.

On my back, I lay
far away from the craze close to where I stay.
I still find a way
to discover a home within this place.

You will never leave me.
In this sacred place, you lead me.
Energy vibrating within every cell of my being.
Equipping me with the love I have always dreamed.

Thank you for being present.
Your love is my greatest lesson.
The teacher that has guided millenniums,
I continue to uplift you as your energy continues
on.

Arise up and throughout the time space continuum.
After the great cleansing you are the residuum.

There is no separation.
We shall never part.
Loving you without any destination,
being that the journey is all in the heart.

369

Throughout the years,
I've learned that love does not just appear
as mere
pulchritude.
For it's always going to be a multitude
of beautiful people scoping you.
But what qualities can they exude, beyond just how
they're viewed?
I sit and ponder
about what it means to open myself up to others.
Letting my mind wander;
I've realized I cannot possess another.
I don't want you as mine,
I want to...
experience your essence in slow motion,
pause time-
unraveling like the kundalini energy throughout my
spine.
Flowing like the river of emotions you possess
within those divine eyes when you're crying.
I embrace your rays in every way you choose to
glow.

Because even on your cloudiest days, you still
managed to create a luminescent rainbow.
The divine alignment that led you to me,
was like the orchestration that Bach channeled
through those keys.
A seraphic symphony playing harmonizing
melodies like English suites.
Do you know me?
In what other dimensions, lifetimes and realms did
we meet?

It is said that 369 holds the answers of time.
So, if I repeat in my mind,
whatever it is, I want to connect with and align,
I can bring it forth within my life?

I am the embodiment of love.
Love is me!
My love does not constrict (3)
I feel free!
I am sagacious with my powers.
I am the master of my Chi!
When I feel gratitude, I feel empowered.
I have all the tools I need in order to succeed!
I speak healing into my DNA (6)

My wellness is guaranteed!

All of my gifts and talents, I embrace;

everything that I want also wants me!

I am constantly protected by love and grace.

I live a wealthy life, full of joy and fulfillment with ease!

Things just keep getting better and better day by day.

I attract all of my desires effortlessly!

I get paid very well to have fun, go out and play.

I now live the life of my dreams. (9)

The Final Act

The final act of love:
asks us to hug.
Brings me right back to us
in this moment's touch.
This woman is running
through the enjoyment of the
smoke–
puffin', blowing marijuana;
damn near
choke-
damn, I want her.
Can't let go...
No.
Please,
don't hold.
I hear you whispering slow.
Kiss me and embrace me
because,
these moments won't last forever.
My heartbeat is racing
because,
what will happen when our lips sever
our bodies are no longer together?

The final act of love:

asks us to let go.

Not in order for us to give up, but to surrender

control.

To take things slow and allow it to unfold,

because

the heart is not looking to be owned,

but to be experienced whole.

Bare witness to the sites left unseen:

it's okay to not know.

Even if you feel like you're not prepared for

everything,

have faith past these fears that you will grow.

Allow this love to be free.

Feel it shifting your soul.

Take reign, your majesty.

Fill my cup until it overflows.

Thank you, eternally my queen.

For now, I know—

love can never truly leave me.

For in my heart, lies its forever home.

Silence Speaks

I wonder...
What is it like to love me too?

I think it feels something like watching those
summertime flowers bloom.
Or like–
having your favorite candy you consume.

Loving me is amazing!

That chasing that turns into an eternal craving.
The pleasure to even taste me?

A delicacy delicately renowned for praising.

It's like falling into the hole within Alice in
wonderland,
where
on one hand,
is this glamorous fantasy
and,
the other
lies demons you can't see.

Because loving me goes far beyond the scenes.

This is not TV, baby: this is reality.

In this ocean of mine,
you'll find
things that will shiver your spine.
Leave you crying
because,
you'll see those parts of me that are slowly dying.

Screaming out in agony
though,
I whisper I'm fine.
Searching for my sanity,
feels like I'm losing my mind.

I,

hold back sometimes, because

I,

don't want you to see me like that.

I,

try to press rewind, but

I,

can never seem to take back time.

The expectations I be placing on
erasing these different phases
got me facing
that I was actually meant to embrace it.

Pausing-
with hesitation
because,
it doesn't make sense.

Tottering on the fence of these feelings, so intense.

How can I love without expectations,
but still
have this bar for my standards that I'm supposed to
be raising?

I don't know what to say.
I be feeling like the world is pulling me in every
different way.

Even as a poet,
and a writer of words...
sometimes I find it
hard to speak pure
truth,
without knowing
these lines that I blur,
choose
where I'm going.
But the guidance ain't there.

Just got to...

breathe in deep and hold on tight.
Pray that ya'
lose no sleep.
Keep ya' peace at night
and I,
got these camels I keep,
When the dessert is dry,

'cause this drought runs deep.
Got no tears left to cry.
Eyes,
filled with beams,
have those dreams
in my mind.
Lie
next to me
if you want to see...
Who am I?

And this
silence, it speaks.

So please, keep quiet.

Acknowledgements

I want to first and foremost thank the creator for being the source of all creation and allowing me to channel so much pure, artistic, loving, creative energy to bring this project to life. Thank you God! To my loving mother, Natalie, for inspiring me and raising me with such strong values to believe I can do and achieve anything I put my mind to. To my amazing father, Lorenzo, for teaching me to take care of what I love and uphold my truth. To my precious Grandmother, whom I call Memmaw, for giving me the blueprint of what pure, unconditional love truly feels like. To my grandparents, Momo and Pawpaw. Momo thank you for showing me what dedication is through your acts of love and discipline in life. Pawpaw, thank you so much for believing in me no matter what. You've played such an important role in my life, not only by encouraging me to follow my dreams but also by supporting me to do so. To my cousins, my little sister, and present family members for gifting me with love and memories I will value for lifetimes. Thank you to all my beloved angels and ancestors, my greats of grandmothers, uncles, cousins, grandfathers and aunts for sending so many divine messages, wisdom, protection and synchronicities that always amaze me and encourage me to keep following my path. To beloved friends, mentors, adventure buddies and students of mine for sharing companionship with me and connections that gave me space to grow. To my first girlfriend Danielle, that showed me what it felt like to be wanted and to be chosen, even if it wasn't reciprocated. Thank you to my ex, Madison for our experience of loving and committing to each other and for awakening so many different parts of myself that I never knew existed before I met you. I truly appreciate our relationship for showing me what it means to choose someone, love them unconditionally and learn to let go, no matter how hard it is. To the beautiful poet, Red Shawty, that inspired Attraction and my first poetry short film. To J, for being such a special friend at such a sensitive time in my life, even when we weren't always on the same page, you reminded me so much of who I am through the chapters we made together. To Michelle, Carolina and Lupita for such genuine, fun friendships and adventures. To Nyjah, for coming back and reminding me that love is magical and all around us, even when we may not be looking for it. To Trashae, for not only playing a role in my first poetry film, but for enlightening me towards a greater form of divinement. To Daralis, for being my mirror and such a powerful catalyst to my rebirth. I am grateful for the pleasure of having been lovers, as our experience together brought such a strong sense of truth and awareness towards the connection with myself and everyone connected to me. To all the people who have been heartbroken, confused, lonely, or lost when it came to love, I dedicate this book to you. May you continue to have the courage to do one of the most extraordinary, bravest things on this planet: love. To generations after me, I want to dedicate this book to you as well. Let my experiences serve as an example of reflection. Take the time to really feel and experience that phenomenal energy that flows to and through us all. Learn it, through the daily practice of choosing yourself and listening to your heart. Find it within you first, so that you may pour endlessly from a spout that never runs out or seeks validation from anyone else. Then, share it and show it to everyone you come into contact with. Infinite love!

About the Author

Afro Hippy

Ahmani Payne is a conscious, love led creator that channels creativity through different art forms. His focus involves empowering creators around the world to live in alignment with their truth. He continues to uplift communities by expressing life through music, *Ahmani's Infinite Love podcast,* short films, poetry and private foundation work.

www.ingramcontent.com/pod-product-compliance
Lightning Source LLC
Chambersburg PA
CBHW020341130626
46549CB00003B/1242